The publishers would like to thank the following Companies for their generous support of this project

HUNTER GARDENS

HUNTER RESORT

McWILLIAMS – MOUNT PLEASANT

PEPPER TREE WINES

ROTHBURY ESTATE

SHAKEY TABLES – HUNTER COUNTRY LODGE

TAMBURLAINE

TOWER ESTATE

TOWER LODGE

HUNTER VALLEY

To: LEON
MERRY CHRISTMAS
2001

From: TOWER ESTATE

166

AUSTRALIAN WINE REGIONS

HUNTER VALLEY

PHOTOGRAPHY BY
R. IAN LLOYD

TEXT BY STEVE ELIAS

EDITED BY WENDY MOORE

R. IAN LLOYD PRODUCTIONS

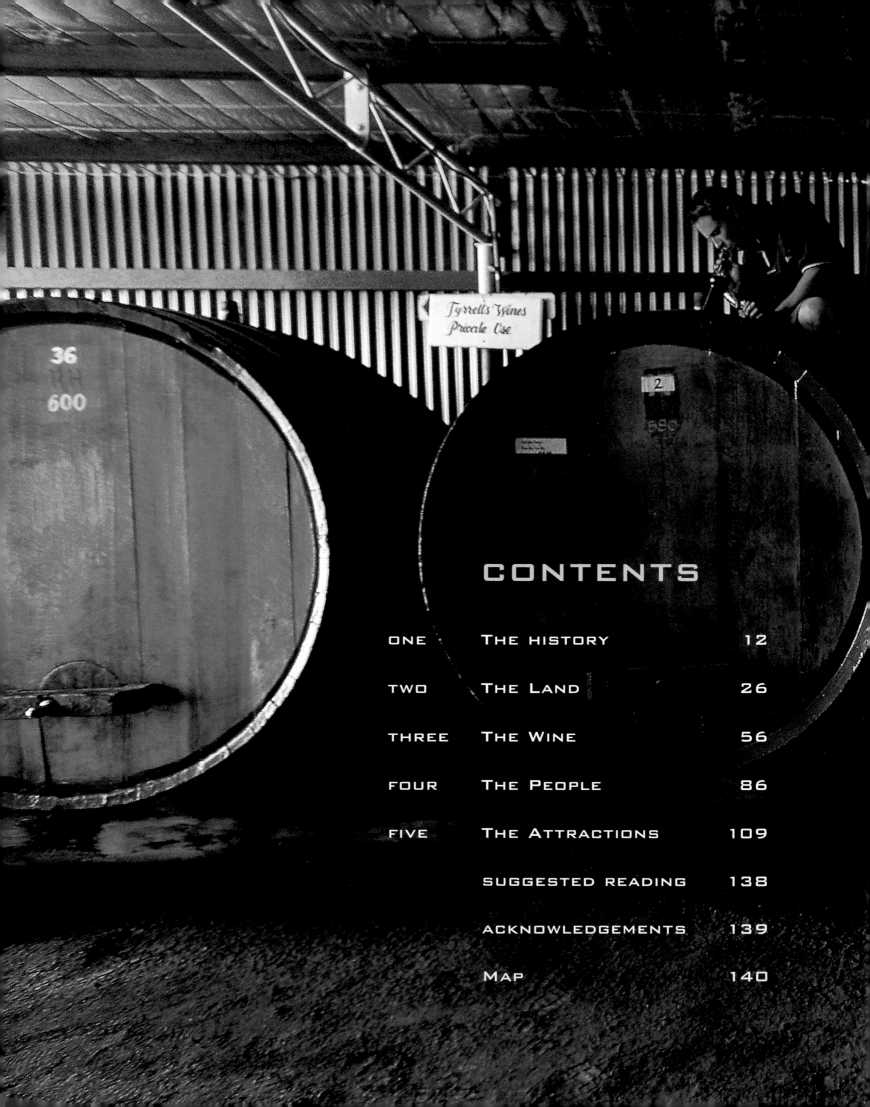

CONTENTS

Previous page: Downstream from the historic river port of Morpeth, a patchwork of paddocks spread across the fertile flood plains at the confluence of the Hunter and Patterson rivers.

This page: The sun dusts the vines of the Scarborough Wine Company with gold as it sets behind the Brokenback Range. *Next page:* The surf rolls in, sculpting the Caves Beach headland at the southern extremity of Seven Mile Beach. To the north is the spectacular Redhead Bluff.

CHAPTER ONE

THE HISTORY

During the Elizabethan period in 16th-century England, there was a strong belief that everything that existed beneath the moon was made from a combination of the four elements: fire, air, water and earth. If all these elements were in balance, then so was the world. If not, discord and conflict would reign.

The story of the Hunter Valley follows the same paradigm. Both Aborigines and Europeans have depended on a harmonious relationship with these elements in order to survive and prosper.

Of the four, however, water has played the most significant role in shaping and moulding the region.

For over 30,000 years before the arrival of the Europeans, the Aboriginal tribes that lived in the region had their own view of the importance of water and its role in the creation of the Valley. They roamed within their tribal territories according to the seasons, living in the closest possible relationship to the land. Particularly in the Lower Hunter, where an abundance of resources made it a land of 'milk and honey'. At Port Stephens, for example, the waters of the bay teemed with fish, the foreshores were covered with oysters and the bush abounded with game and wild fruits.

Unfortunately, it was also water that was the catalyst for their demise for, in 1787, the First Fleet sailed from England to this island continent to dispatch its cargo of convicts. It would be another ten years, however, before their paradise would be lost forever.

The fateful day arrived on September 9, 1797, when Lieutenant John Shortland, on his return from a futile search for escaped convicts, entered a river mouth that the local Aborigines knew as the Coquon, and named it after Governor Hunter. It was a significant discovery, but the young lieutenant was to make an even more important discovery. "In this harbour," he related, "was found a very considerable quantity of coal of a very good sort, and lying so near the water side as to be conveniently shipped." One year later, Shortland wrote these prophetic words to his father in England: "I daresay in a very little time this river will be a very great acquisition to the settlement."

As the colony of New South Wales expanded, further exploration took place under the command of Lieutenant Colonel Paterson, who charted the harbour and the river, including two

This historic photograph shows the *Lucy A. Nickles* tied up at Newcastle's Queens Wharf in November 1890 (*opposite*). The image of Baiame (*above*), the creator and protector of the Aboriginal people, is painted on the walls of a cave near Milbrodale, the arms outstretched as if embracing an image of the land.

This section of an aquatint by Joseph Lycett, the twice-convicted forger, depicts Aborigines resting by a campfire near the mouth of the Hunter River in 1817. In the background is Nobby's Island, before it was connected to the mainland. Lycett's *Views of Australia* were idealized pictures that made the harsh Australian landscape look like the well-ordered, neatly landscaped park an English nobleman might own.

of its main tributaries, the Williams and Paterson and, on his advice, a settlement was established at the mouth of the Hunter. This proved to be a failure, but with the local resources of cedar and coal to rely on, a second and successful attempt was made in 1804. This new settlement, named Kingstown after the new Governor, now became a gaol for the colony's worst offenders.

In those early days of Newcastle (as it was later named), cedar gangs moved further into the hinterland, as the good stands of timber were cut from the areas around the river. These extensive forests of red cedar *(Toona ciliata)* were then thought to be inexhaustible. Before the axemen came, the giant red cedar and fig trees bore their tall trunks upward through the myrtle and other softwoods, crowning all with their wide-spreading canopies.

It was an impressive sight, as a European visitor in 1818 observed: "The scenery on the banks of these rivers is very fine; some parts being low and thickly wooded, while other parts present to the view sloping banks, luxuriant herbage, and majestic trees, scattered in beautiful profusion, and assuming the appearance of a gentleman's park in England ... When this land is granted, it is likely to become one of the most fertile settlements in the colony, as the soil is rich and free from floods, and the navigation good for 60 miles."

However, until overland routes from Sydney were established, few free settlers went to the

Hunter Valley. John Howe, Chief Constable of Windsor, took the lead in 1819, when he blazed a trail between the Hawkesbury and the Hunter rivers, and four years later a convict-built road was established along his path. Then, in 1825, the surveyor Henry Finch, cut a shorter and less arduous route to Maitland, which became the Great Northern Road. This was the major artery along which the free settlers moved to establish themselves on the upper creeks of the Wollombi, where cedar and rosewood forests were being exploited. And, in time, wheat, tobacco, butter, beef, barley, oats and wine were produced on the pioneers' farms.

No one knows who planted the first vines. Popular opinion suggests it was William Kelman, brother-in-law to the founder of the Australian wine industry, James Busby, who had been granted 2,000 acres on the Hunter River between Singleton and Branxton in 1824, naming it Kirkton, after his birthplace.

James Busby was a visionary whose main reason for promoting winemaking was "to increase the comforts, and promote the morality of the lower classes of the Colony." The idea was to destroy the rum monopoly and its "mischievous results". But, his pragmatism was tempered by 19th-century Romanticism. As he wrote: "The man who could sit under the shade of his own vine, with his wife and children about him, and the ripe clusters hanging within their reach, in such a climate as this, and not feel the

One of the earliest guns installed at Fort Scratchley is depicted in this photograph from around 1888. Named after Major General Peter Scratchley of the Royal Engineers, the fort was built as part of the colonial government's defence system and stands guard at the entrance to the Hunter River.

Another pioneer grape-grower was George Wyndham. At his Dalwood property near Branxton he produced his first vintage in 1835. But it was plagued by problems, causing George to remark that, "it should make good vinegar". Penfolds acquired his vineyard in 1904, turning Dalwood into a national brand. This same property is now called Wyndham Estate.

Busby's property at Kirkton was an inspiration to many other viticulturists, including Doctor Lindeman, a surgeon who migrated to Australia in 1840. Lindeman settled at Gresford on the Paterson River where he opened a medical practice. Two years later he acquired the Cawarra Estate and quickly established a reputation for producing wines of very good quality. Even when his winery was destroyed by fire, he worked in the Victorian gold fields to restore his lost fortunes, returned to the Hunter and applied his business acumen, setting up a bottling plant in the Queen Victoria Building in Sydney.

After Doctor Lindeman's death in 1881, his son Charles continued the company's rapid expansion, buying several famous vineyards and wineries, such as Wilkinson's Coolalta and the Ben Ean winery, which was bought in 1912. In time, Lindemans was to become an international brand.

Another pioneer who did much to improve both the quality of Hunter grapes and publicity for its wines was James King. At his property Irrawang near Raymond Terrace, he encouraged larger plantings, improved quality control and was instrumental in founding the influential Hunter River Vineyard Association in 1847. He was one of the first to export his wines to

Sydney photographer Max Dupain was commissioned in the late 1940s and early '50s to take a series of photographs in the Hunter to illustrate winemaking, viticulture and the people of an era now replaced by advanced technology.

highest enjoyment, is incapable of happiness, and does not know what the word means."

In 1831 Busby travelled to England and the vineyards of France and Spain, returning to Sydney the following year with several hundred cuttings. These he planted at Kirkton where they apparently thrived.

Britain, and one of these, probably a Semillon, won a medal at the Paris Exhibition in 1855 and was placed on the table of Napoleon III.

At that stage, the principal grapes grown in the Hunter were semillon, black hamburg and lambruscat. In 1860, Hunter wine production was more than 60,000 gallons (270,000 litres), and although this was an impressive amount for a young, non-wine producing country, it is only about ten percent of The Rothbury Estate's present annual production.

In fact, at that time, wine was not the most popular alcoholic beverage. Rum at threepence a glass led the field then at half the price of brandy, wine or ale. Wine, probably sweet and fortified, was four and sixpence a bottle – extremely expensive, considering that a loaf of bread cost a penny or so.

The tyranny of distance was also a significant factor. There was no rail link to Sydney until the 1880s, and as the roads were rough and unsuited for wine carting, farmers relied heavily on shipping. Produce was taken by riverboats to Morpeth for transshipment to the more economical coastal steamers, as at that time, the Hunter River was navigable beyond Singleton. Morpeth then was the hub of the Hunter Valley. The town throbbed with activity, its wharves lined with great sailing ships and paddle steamers loading wool, wheat, timber, wine and tobacco.

All the early vineyards had been established north of the Hunter River, between Raymond Terrace and Singleton, but soon they spread to the south, away from the river and on to the slopes of the Brokenback Range. In the 1860s, they extended to Lochinvar and Allandale with names such as Joseph Holmes and George Campbell being prominent.

Pokolbin, currently the centre of the Lower Hunter wine region, was born in 1866 when the Wilkinson family, considered by the wine writer James Halliday to be, "the most dominant force among the wine-growing families of the 19th century", took up several parcels of land along the foothills of the Brokenback Range. These parcels became Oakdale, Cote d'Or, Mangerton, Maluna and Coolalta.

The next few years were very prosperous for the Hunter, with an area of between 500 and 1,000 acres under vines, and 168,123 gallons of wine being produced in 1866.

Dupain said of these photographs, "The wine photos have been reduced to a simple format – not over complicated and with very little intellectual content. It's purely visual, optical and emotional."

At 10.27am on 28 December 1989, an earthquake measuring 5.6 on the Richter scale shook the city of Newcastle. The quake killed 13 people and thousands of buildings were damaged. The city's emergency services faced an uphill battle in dealing with devastation immediately following the main shock.

As transport improved, so did sales. In the early 1900s, the shared cellars of Lindemans and Penfolds in Sydney's Queen Victoria Building were claimed to be, "the largest city cellars in the world underground".

Unfortunately, the honeymoon was about to end. The bank crash and recession of the 1890s, combined with the removal of customs barriers, following Federation, which allowed cheaper South Australian wines to enter New South Wales, had a dramatic impact. However, the ultimate blow came in 1917 with the appearance in the Hunter of the vine disease, downy mildew. The damage this caused was substantial, with three-quarters of the 1925 crop lost to the disease. Many pioneering families were forced to sell out, thus bringing to an end the first Hunter wine rush.

century." The son of a French mother and an Irish father, Maurice studied winemaking in France. He returned to Australia in 1921 and took over as winemaker four years later, renaming the vineyard Mount Pleasant.

At a time when the Hunter Valley was going through a period of rapid decline, O'Shea became something of a legend. For 40 years he grew and bought wines for blending into masterpieces. Max Lake, wine writer and winemaker, wrote that O'Shea's success with wine was in part due to the fact that he was a true artist: "He used wines like a painter uses colour and textures."

The McWilliam family bought Mount Pleasant in the early 1930s, retaining O'Shea as winemaker, thus saving the operation from possible collapse during the Depression. But, ironically, it was those hard times that laid the foundations for the Hunter's revival, for in order to survive, many small producers sold their wine in bulk to be bottled by other wine producers or merchants. One of these merchants was Leo Buring, who had been a winemaker, wine consultant, restaurateur and manager for Lindemans. He bottled wine from producers, such as Draytons and Elliots, under his own label and distributed them nationally. The other important merchant was Johnny Walker. Also a restaurateur, he sold wine under the Rhinecastle label, much of which was supplied by Tulloch's, whose reputation he helped to establish. And, although the Hunter wine industry remained stagnant until the early 1960s, these and other merchants were sowing the seeds for Australians to develop a love for wine.

It can be argued that the second Hunter wine rush began in 1963 when Dr Max Lake

With vineyard acreage declining and prices falling, the climate for change was ripe Penfolds purchased John Wyndham's original Dalwood property, beginning a fertile 70-year association with the region, and the O'Shea's bought Mount View vineyard, which had been established in 1880 by Charles King. This latter purchase was a turning point, as James Halliday remarked: "with Maurice O'Shea we come fairly into the 20th started Lakes Folly, which according to wine writer Nick Bulleid, was "the first new winery in living memory". Max was a Macquarie Street surgeon, author and *bon vivant* who'd had an epiphany when drinking a 1934 Cabernet Verdot grown at Dalwood. He started his vineyard, planting Cabernet Sauvignon, to hopefully recreate a great Hunter wine, but in the process opened the door to others, such as Jim Roberts at Belbourie, David Horden with Brogheda and Dr Lance Allen at Tamburlaine who, with money and passion, also took up the challenge and reinvented the Hunter.

Following close on their heels were larger concerns who perceived a sea change taking place. Hungerford Hill Vineyards had planted about 240 hectares by 1970, and the Rothbury Estate, a concept created by Len Evans, had 320 hectares, with its four main vineyards: Rothbury, Brokenback, Homestead Hill and Herlstone.

Another entrepreneur was ex-Penfold's winemaker Brian McGuigan. In 1971, he formed Wyndham Estate with other investors, purchased the old Dalwood Estate from his father Perc and proceeded to revolutionize the marketing of wine. Brian understood what the average wine drinker wanted and he supplied them. By the late 1980s, Wyndham Estate had grown to be one of the largest brands in Australia and was also making a big noise internationally.

Built in 1870, the National Trust property, Grossman House, is furnished as a Victorian merchant's town house. This substantial two-storey building, reflects the business success of merchant and entrepreneur Isaac Beckett.

It was, however, the Upper Hunter that laid claim to the largest vineyard. In the early 1970s, Arrowfield boasted 480 hectares, with other vineyards in this region, such as Richmond Grove and Rosemount, also making an impact. By 1976 there were over 4,000 hectares of vineyards in the Hunter. The phoenix had surely risen.

With the industry firmly replanted in the Hunter, consumers changed their preference from red to white wine, causing another shuffling of the cards. But by the 1980s, the region began to consolidate.

The next major change was the tourist boom of the 1990s. The proximity to Sydney has changed the face of the Hunter Valley. Vineyards of the '70s, which metarmorphosized into wineries in the '80s, matured into accommodation houses, art galleries and cellar doors in the '90s and into the new century. Restaurants, cafes, art galleries and extreme sports all compete to attract the tourist dollar. The result is that the Hunter Valley is now Sydney's gastronomic theme park.

Also, contract winemaking and a new professionalism in viticulture have made the agricultural side more accessible, but marketing the ever increasing number of labels is still the most difficult aspect to master.

With the influx of so much new investment, land values in the Pokolbin region have skyrocketed, pushing the newer vineyards into wider orbits, west to the Broke Fordwich area, east to Lovedale and south along the Wollombi Brook. Although the traditional vignerons are enjoying the benefits that the new money is bringing, there is a latent fear that this bubble may also burst.

But the Hunter Valley continues to reinvent itself. As in Elizabethan England, there is a renaissance, an awakening to the ability to use the heritage of the past and combine it with the region's own native gifts and products to produce a prosperous future.

Maitland presents a legacy of the 19th-century colonial period with stately mansions, grand civic buildings and churches.

The Singleton Courthouse (*top*), an example of the mid-Victorian Italianate architectural style, was designed by colonial architect James Barnet. Built in 1868, it reflects the economic confidence associated with the coming of the railway to Singleton in 1863. The Church of St. Matthias at Denman (*above*), completed in 1875, is a lively and decorative example of John Horbury Hunt's Neo-Gothic country church. The architectural monuments of the coalfields are the pitheads and the hotels. The latter are vast and reflect Edwardian prosperity. Amongst the best examples is the Kurri Kurri Hotel (*opposite*).

CHAPTER TWO

THE LAND

In the Aboriginal Dreamtime, there once was a greedy little frog called Tittalik. One day he decided to drink up all the water out of the pools and springs. He drank and drank, growing bigger and bigger, until there was no water left for the other animals. In desperation they called a meeting and agreed that if Tittalik opened his mouth for long enough, the water would spill out. Someone suggested, "Make him laugh!"

First the Emu tried but he did not succeed, then the Kangaroo, but he also failed. All the animals tried but none of them could make the frog laugh. They were just about to give up when along came the Platypus, who began to walk up the hill towards Tittalik. But on the way up he tripped over a rock and tumbled back down. Then he picked himself up, and again started climbing, only to roll back down the hill.

All of a sudden the Kookaburra started laughing and one by one the other animals joined in. The laughter became so infectious that eventually Tittalik began to laugh. He laughed and laughed and all the water from the pools and springs gushed out of his mouth and down the hill. Finally, the water came to rest in a gully, and became a great river. This is how the Hunter began.

Its catchment, the Hunter Valley, on Australia's eastern coast, is a unique and amazingly diversified region, unified by the river and enclosed on three sides by mountains, which stretch almost to the sea. It covers an area of about 28,000 square kilometres and forms a complete physical, social and economic unit encompassing primary, secondary and tertiary industries.

Beneath the Hunter's mosaic of rich alluvial plains, rolling hills and dramatic mountains, lie massive coal measures, the foundation of its industrial development – and the source of the Hunter's early name – Coal River.

The Hunter River rises in the Barrington Tops, gathers in the Pages and its tributaries, and flows southwest to Denman, where it is joined by the Goulburn River. From this junction, the Hunter flows eastward to the sea at Nobby's, joined on its way by Wollombi Brook above Singleton, and the Paterson and Williams rivers below Maitland.

The western boundary of the Hunter Valley catchment is the Great Dividing Range which,

Rising with the morning sun (*opposite*), a passenger in a hot air balloon catches a glimpse of the natural beauty of the Pokolbin district and the Brokenback Range. The lush rainforest surrounding Jerusalem Creek is home to delicate tree ferns (*above*).

at this point, is unusually low, its forested undulating sandstone country scored by narrow gullies. In contrast, the northeastern portion of the Valley, bounded by the Mount Royal Range, is mountainous, rugged country.

Barrington Tops, the highest plateau at over 1,650 metres above sea level, extends between a series of extinct volcanic peaks in the Mount Royal Ranges. On this 25-kilometre-long plateau, 80 kilometres west of the coast, alpine fields, saturated with wildflowers in spring, spread out beneath the stunted, silver-beige trunks of the snow gums. Fields of bluebells, yellow-and-white paper daisies, slender rice flowers and yellow billy buttons flower between the grey-green snow grass and the rush-like lomandra with its orange seeds that the Aborigines once ground for flour.

The melting snow, which is often heavy enough for skiing, flows down to the sea through ancient beech forests immersed in an eerie emerald glow. Pure, clear water runs from sphagnum moss swamps fed by an annual rainfall exceeding 1,500 millimetres.

More than 20 valleys radiate from the plateau. Waterfalls plunge into fern-lined gorges and in the river valleys of the lowlands, weathered basalt, washed down from the mountains, forms rich alluvial soils.

The rainforest in Barrington Tops National Park is the southernmost link in a chain of remnant rainforests throughout central eastern Australia. Here, Antarctic beech forests cloak the slopes above the 900-metre mark, which are crowded with tree ferns and sassafras. In spring, the fieldia, a fragile vine with tiny scalloped leaves, glows with showers of bell-like flowers and orchids cascade their creamy-white sprays from beech boughs.

Further down the slopes, warm-temperate rainforest species merge with wet-eucalypt forest species such as tallow-wood, stringy barks, blue gums and rough-barked angophoras. On arid slopes dry eucalypts thrive, and adjacent to the subalpine swamps and woodlands, grassy summits known as 'grassland balds' cap the summits.

The remarkable range of habitats found in the Barrington Tops nurtures half the plant species found in Australia and over one third of its mammals and birds. There is a high concentration of gliders and owls, including the barking owl, which emits a blood-curdling, human-like scream while hunting at night. The powerful masked and sooty owls, however, join 23 other animals on the endangered list, including the koala, tiger quoll, red-legged pademelon, yellow-bellied glider, broad-toothed rat and sphagnum frog. It is also home to one of Australia's rarest birds, the tiny and elusive rufous scrub bird, as well as the magnificent,

The Pines Forest Park in the Watagan State Forest is set amongst large slash pine trees which are remnants of trial plantings of different pine species established during the 1920s and 1930s.

iridescent blue-green paradise riflebird, which belongs to the birds-of-paradise family.

In the Gloucester Tops, the subalpine woodlands are home to grey kangaroos, swamp wallabies, pademelons, common wombats and red-necked wallabies. The rare and endangered eastern native cat is sometimes seen in similar habitats. Birds most commonly observed include the raucous yellow-tailed black cockatoo, the endearing scarlet robin, spotted pardalote and eastern whipbird.

The Allyn and Williams Rivers drop off sharply from the easterly peaks of the Barrington Tops, rushing down rocky riverbeds, through fern-lined banks where platypuses can sometimes

be seen, resting in pools beside the riverbank. The subtropical rainforest here abounds in wildlife, and red cedars and strangler figs are common. The state's largest river oak can also be found here.

Coal lies beneath this region too. It manifests itself in the fantastic Burning Mountain, at Wingen, where the thick coal seams of the Greta series have been on fire for thousands of years, ignited possibly from heat generated by oxidation of sulphur, perhaps by a burning tree falling across a coal outcrop. Sometimes smoke erupting from the hillside can be seen for a great distance. In this dangerous area, where a false step can send the unwary hurtling

This vista looks south from Caves Beach along the rugged coastline towards the historic mining village and surfing mecca of Catherine Hill Bay.

In the early morning and just on dusk, kangaroos venture out onto the open paddocks to graze on the new green shoots and quench their thirst in the dams that dot the landscape.

into blazing underground caverns, sheep have been known to stumble down the cracks and be roasted alive.

The story of coal in the Valley goes back 28,000-million years, to the period known by geologists as the Permian, which lasted for 30-million years. Throughout this time, the nexus of climate and vegetation was ideal for coal formation. Layer upon layer of plants grew and died in the shallow acidic water of the Hunter's swamps, compressing into peat — the first stage in the formation of coal. The 250-million years from the end of the Permian to the present provided the other ingredients — time, pressure and heat. Today, the underground and open cut

mines of the Hunter valley produce more than 60-million tonnes of coal every year.

On the southern side of the Hunter Valley, bordered by the Watagan Mountains, is the cul-de-sac known as the Cessnock-Wollombi region. Its mountains are clothed in wet sclerophyll forest, home to smooth-barked blue gums, mahogany and turpentine, the latter often providing shelter for the bell miner, or 'bellbirds', that are often heard but seldom seen. Also growing here are grey-brown blackbutt, whose flowers are much sought after by flying foxes, lorikeets and honeyeaters.

In the understorey, the lovely forest oak with its cork-like bark, shares space with the dense-

On the narrow, stony ridges of the Watagan State Forest, blackboys share the skeletal
soils with bladey grass and lilies, tick bush, woody pear and the occasional waratah.

crowned kurrajong with its bell-shaped flowers, as well as yellow-flowered dogwoods. On the forest floor, the unique bonnet orchid pollinates by fooling the male wasp into mating with its flowers, which emit the scent of the female wasp. Also found here are large, translucent-green bird's-nest ferns, bulbous elkhorns clinging to rocks and trees, native holly, wild raspberry, orange thorn and the crimson-flowered Waratah, the floral emblem of New South Wales.

As the mountains descend into the steep-sided valleys of Wollombi Brook and Wollombi Creek the vegetation changes. Rough-skinned iron barks and smooth-barked spotted gums attract galahs and crested pigeons from the inland, while the streams in the valley floor are fringed by pine-like river oaks.

On the opposite side of this region is the aptly named Brokenback Range, guarding the vineyards of Pokolbin and Broke like an immense, sleeping dragon. In its forests grow the yellow bloodwood with its scaly, pale-yellow skin, the peppermint, the apple gum and the rare Pokolbin mallee. Bush lilies share the forest floor with the woody pear and grass trees like the blackboys.

About 20 different kinds of bats call the Hunter Valley their home. Some, such as the eastern horseshoe and the bent-winged, prefer to roost in caves or old mine shafts during the day, taking over the 'night shift' to hunt for insects.

There are many ground-dwelling mammals that have adapted to life in the region's forests. The red-necked and swamp wallabies are still common in parts of the Lower Hunter, but much rarer is the brush-tailed rock wallaby. These are found in isolated colonies, usually in rugged and inaccessible country such as the Watagans. Smoky grey wallaroos will venture out from the security of the bush to feed on open grazing land, while grey kangaroos prefer gentler terrain with grassy clearings and a regular water supply that the valleys of the Upper Hunter provide. Pademelons, dumpy, dark-coloured wallabies, are also common in the gullies of the Watagans.

The Watagans also provide a backdrop to Lake Macquarie, the southern coastal limit of the Hunter. One of the largest coastal lakes in Australia, it covers an area of approximately 110-square kilometres with a catchment that supports a wide range of habitats and offers extraordinary biodiversity.

Just below the lake's surface seagrasses thrive, providing cover for prawns, crabs and young fish to hide from predators. The seagrass supports leatherjacket, blackfish and mullet, which in turn feed a surprising assortment of birds. The stately black and white jabiru, pelicans, black swans, white egrets and white-faced herons all share the resources of the lake.

South of the lake's entrance at Swansea Heads, lies Caves Beach, the southern end of 13 kilometres of sand that ends at the dramatic weather-sculptured headland of Redhead beach. This stretch of coastline is often littered with coal, which has been washed up on the sand, a reminder of the region's geological history.

The beaches continue north to the landmark of Nobby's Head, standing vigil at the entrance to the Hunter River at Newcastle. The harbour mouth is flanked by a collection of city beaches,

Ferns are fussy plants, requiring shelter from the wind, shade and high humidity. These delicate green laces grow close to the ground in places like the Barrington Tops.

cupped between the headlands of Nobby's, Newcastle, Shepherd's Hill and Merewether to the immediate south.

Across the harbour from the city, the suburb of Stockton lies on a bed of sand, supplemented with ballast delivered from the holds of tall ships. To the north is the remarkable Stockton Bight, 30 kilometres of sand dunes that run to the headlands of the northern boundary of the region, Port Stephens.

Dominated by the towering peaks of Tomaree and Yaccaba, Port Stephens abounds in fish and birdlife. Beyond its backwaters lie the fertile banks of the Karuah, Williams and Hunter rivers, while to the south, hugging the ocean along the Stockton Peninsula, white, sandy beaches are backed by rugged bushland.

All the Hunter's natural splendour is attributed in Aboriginal legend to the great spirit Baiame, who divided the land into tribal boundaries using landforms such as rivers and mountains. Baiame then became the keeper of the Valley, and nowhere is this legend better understood than in the peaceful serenity of a little cave at Milbrodale where an Aboriginal rock painting depicts Baiame. With arms outstretched, this ancient image appears to be embracing the land.

From the earliest European contact there has been extensive land use in the Hunter, but fortunately large areas of natural vegetation, that provide sanctuary for the native fauna, have survived. With more vigilance and care, Baiame may well have reason to smile again.

The rural idyll looking back from Pokolbin Mountain road shows lush paddocks clothing the fertile red clay loam that predominates in this area.

The mist rises over the vineyards of the Broke/Fordwich Valley. This region is based on the sandy river flats and red clay slopes alongside the Wollombi Brook. The climate here is a little warmer and drier than Pokolbin and avoids some of the summer rainfall that plagues the rest of the Lower Hunter.

Like dinosaur skeletons (*opposite*), the power grid marches across the valley taking electricity from the power stations in the Upper Hunter to the National Grid. Early morning fogs (*above*) are common in the Lower Hunter, promising beautiful, crystal clear days with deep blue skies and high summer temperatures, tempered by sea breezes. Southerly busters, squalls and cold fronts visit the region regularly, providing spectacular and often damaging storms.

According to some of the local old timers, the best time to see the magnificent Pool of Reflections (*above*), on the Williams River in the Barrington Tops, is in the morning light. Sometimes the pools are filled with gravel by violent floods and then perhaps the next flood will clear them again. The Slippery Dip (*right*), also on the Williams River, is an excellent spot for sliding and swimming. Descending to the Slippery Dip, you may feel a change in the air, and notice that it is not so humid. The river creates an opening in the forest, allowing a passage for air, water and sunlight.

The 35,000-hectare Barrington Tops National Park is located on the eastern escarpment of the Great Dividing Range. It contains two linked plateaus, Barrington and Gloucester Tops, and the headwaters of several rivers. The climate is cool in summer with cold, wet winters. The plateaus are undulating with their edges incised by rivers forming deep chasms. Sub-alpine woodlands are the major environments on the plateau. On the sheltered slopes along the creeks are cool temperature rainforests, while warm temperature subtropical rainforests occur in the valleys along the lower sections of the Allyn, Patterson, Chichester and Williams rivers.

Jerusalem Creek is in the foothills of the Barrington Tops National Park in the Chichester State Forest. Elkhorns and other epiphytes, mosses, lichens, vines and ferns abound and there is an old axe-cut log from pre-chainsaw days, an old and narrow bullock track from pre-bulldozer days and a crop of blue gums.

Previous page: The Jerusalem Creek Walking Trail makes its way from an area of dry eucalypt forest down into a gully where the ecosystem undergoes a transition to moist sclerophyll forest. It finishes at Jerusalem Creek Forest Park where the magnificent Jerusalem Creek Falls cascade down between banks of lush forest in a protected area of the Chichester State Forest.

This spectacular panorama of the Hunter Valley (*left*) is from the Eaglereach Wilderness Resort, perched precariously on a ridge that separates the Upper Hunter from the Barrington Tops and the coastal strip to the east. A classic rural scene (*above*) is captured near Dungog, located in a valley surrounded by rolling hills adjacent to the Williams River. The rusting corrugated iron sheds, the creek meandering down through the slopes to join the river and the irrigated paddocks on the river flats are typical of the Hunter Valley.

Layers of colour and form belie the function of the Woodlands Stud Farm, one of the horse studs that operate near Denman, on the rim of the Upper Hunter Valley. What was once an area known for its horse and cattle studs has recently seen a veritable explosion of vineyards as more people take advantage of the Australian wine boom.

Morpeth (*left*) is an historic inland river port with a bucolic feel on the banks of the Hunter River. With its beautiful riverside setting, the genuinely historic atmosphere that emerges from the mellowed stonework of its many old buildings, and the willows which line the riverbank, has made it popular with travellers. The paddocks fan out from the banks of the Hunter River (*above*) as it meanders on its journey to the sea at Newcastle. Once the main highway into the valley, it is still the major artery that feeds the farms.

"The land held the key to life's secrets. Man was given the knowledge to read the land and for every rock, tree and creek he found an explanation for existence. He did not own the land, the land owned him. To know the land was to know life." An extract from James Miller's, *Koori: A Will To Win*.

A moment for reflection at the end of the day by a dam below the Graveyard block of the Brokenwood Winery. Named after this piece of land in Pokolbin, Brokenwood's Graveyard shiraz is considered one of the Hunter's outstanding wines with ripe, plummy flavours wrapped in a blanket of toasty oak.

CHAPTER THREE

THE WINE

Len Evans, the renowned guru of Australian wine, fondly remembers his first encounter with the Hunter Valley: "When I first came here in 1959, on an extremely hot day, it took over five hours to get here from Sydney ... Tullochs was the main winery at that stage. Lindemans and McWilliams were bigger but you had to have permission to go there and they didn't sell wine, Tullochs did.

"I can remember having grilled crayfish, cooked outside on a wood fire. It was so hot, I think it was 105°(F), and we had beakers of white wine with ice in them and soda because it was just too hot to drink wine. But I loved the place, because it was a true, extremely simple, wine district."

In this recollection Len really put his finger on a number of elements that characterize Australia's oldest winemaking region: the climate, the winemakers, the wine, the proximity to Sydney and, of course, the food.

The macroclimate of a wine region governs whether it is capable of producing ripe wine grapes at all, while the subtle characteristics of a much smaller area – a particular vineyard for example – may determine the sort of wine that can be produced from it. These characteristics

include the climate, its soils, the lie of the land, and the effects each of these three elements have on each other. The French, typically, have one elegant word for this long list of natural characteristics: *terroir*.

Most vignerons would agree that the Hunter is not the perfect place to grow grapes. Soil types allow only low vigour and yields, and rainfall is at a seasonal low in late winter and spring, exactly when you most need it.

Three months rainfall can flood the area over the harvest period in summer, and hail can also decimate crops at the same time. Despite this, however, the terroir of the Hunter produces two major grape varieties – semillon and shiraz – and these are converted into two of the most distinctive and superb wine styles in Australia.

Semillon is the great white grape of sweet white bordeaux, responsible for Bordeaux's greatest dry whites and Australia's most distinctive table wine, Hunter Valley Semillon. This renowned wine is light, crisp, delicate and intense, and it can even show aromatic characters. However, leave the wine in the bottle for at least four years and it transforms into a soft, richly flavoured wine, unrecognizable from its modest beginning.

Summer is the busy season in the Hunter Valley as the vineyards prepare for vintage in early February. Much of the warmth the Hunter gets for ripening the grapes is early in the season, which gives the vines a quick start.

Maurice O'Shea (the legendary McWilliams's winemaker) and it was still in perfect condition. Delicious wine."

Shiraz is the Australian (and South African) name for the original French variety syrah. Widely planted in Australia, shiraz cuttings were imported by wine pioneer James Busby from Montpellier in France in 1832. The variety was immediately successful and spread rapidly.

Shiraz is versatile – it prefers warm climates but is successful in very hot as well as quite cold locations. Hunter shiraz is medium, even light-bodied, but ages well and can live a long time. Wines made by Maurice O'Shea in the 1940s and '50s are still discussed with awe. Back then, conditions were primitive, and cooling the ferment consisted of dumping ice blocks into it. The Hunter pioneers such as Tyrrell's, McWilliams's Mt Pleasant, Lindemans and Tulloch made their names with shiraz.

Primitive conditions, the use of open ferments, and the heat, led to a consistent sulphide character on the reds. It was often a balanced part of the wine and was described as a leathery or 'sweaty saddle' character which was thought to be inherent in the Hunter. However, in the last two decades, winemaking in the Hunter Valley, and everywhere else, has modernized and the leathery flavour has disappeared. Hunter reds are earthy with a red-berry flavour tinged with spicy-pepper, and overall are medium to light-bodied compared to other Australian reds.

By mid-2001 there were 43 wineries and 160 grape growers in the Lower Hunter centred around Pokolbin, and 12 more wineries and 20 grape growers in the Upper Hunter. The

Peter Charteris, the winemaker at Brokenwood, practising the traditional Burgundian method of lees stirring, or batonnage, to encourage extra layers of flavour and minimize the wine's absorption of harsh tannins and flavour from the wood in the barrel.

"Semillon is not only the great idiosyncratic wine of Australia, but also of the Hunter Valley," observes Len Evans. "I know Semillon backwards. I used to have a vineyard in Bordeaux, where we grew Semillon. I've never seen a Bordeaux wine near as good as a Hunter and these wines have this incredible propensity to age. I recently opened my last 1953 Florence Semillon from proximity of Sydney, Australia's major global city, has been a critical influence on the area's investments in wine production and, more recently, its emergence as Australia's premier wine-and-food landscape.

The quintessential image of a Hunter winemaker is based on a local rural family and its pioneer roots with the surviving patriarch as chief winemaker. It is an image that is firmly projected by the Hunter's medium-sized family companies: Draytons, McGuigan Brothers, McWilliams, Rosemount and Tyrrell's.

A case in point is Murray Tyrrell, the patriarch of Australia's largest family-operated winery, who died in October 2000, aged 79. Murray was born into a winemaking family, with his father Avery teaching him viticulture, while his uncle Dan was his instructor in winemaking. Uncle Dan, who made wine for a record 75 vintages before his death in 1959, was acknowledged as a great maker of red wine.

Tyrrell's Wines found its edge in producing top quality semillon and distinctive shiraz, and through Murray's foresight, one of Australia's best chardonnays. In fact, his good friend Len Evans, the founder of Rothbury Estate, and more recently Tower Estate, introduced him to chardonnay. "Len taught me about drinking fine wine," he once said. "He often produced some of the world's great chardonnays and that influenced me to grow it."

In 1973, with brand new Nevers oak barrels, Murray fermented and then matured his first wooded chardonnay. The 1973 Vat 47 chardonnay went on to win a championship, a trophy and ten gold medals. It was also Murray's favourite wine.

Murray's son Bruce, the general manager of the company, admits that they were a lucky family, right from the beginning: "By coming late in 1858, 30 years after the first grapes were planted, we ended up a significant distance from Maitland, the hub of the area, with land under the mountain. Under the mountain you've got limestone, so it was a lucky accident." Lucky, because limestone soils produce excellent quality grapes.

This selection of Hunter Valley wines is available from the unique cellar of Simon Rennger at Shakey Tables Restaurant.

Bruce is committed to the quality of his wine and is determined that the great styles of the region are preserved and not lost. "You have to maintain your heritage," he insists.

The Hunter's national and international exposure as a winemaking region hinges, to a large degree, on Murray Tyrrell's contribution to wine tourism, as well as the larger-than-life figure of Brian McGuigan, the managing director of McGuigans Wines. A more enthusiastic and passionate person would be hard to find, especially when it comes to wine in general and the Hunter Valley in particular.

Brian, with his wife Fay, have seen the highs and lows of the wine industry. From creating Wyndham Estate in 1970 and watching it grow over 19 years to be one of the largest brands in Australia, and making big inroads into international markets, to the devastation of it being taken over by the French liquor group Pernod Ricard during a turbulent period of his life, and then having to rebuild his empire.

Brian began as a trainee in 1960, at Penfolds. As he recalls, "I started as a winemaker and viticulturist but I quickly learnt that I had to become a lot more than that. At Wyndham Estate, we had to develop product and I had to learn to market. That's what we did, and we did it well."

As everybody in Pokolbin was growing mainly shiraz and semillon, Brian wondered how he could compete against people like Lindeman's, McWilliams, Tyrrell's and Draytons, who had been doing it so well with old

wines for so long. His solution was to develop a blend of Traminer and Riesling, which he felt would hit the spot with consumers. It was an instant hit. " I put the whole future of Wyndham Estate on Traminer Riesling," he admits. "After that, we had a reputation for being commercial, but really, it was the right thing to do. We did that fruity thing, but then we came out with the Chablis Superior, the driest white wine on the Australian market, followed by 444 the most intense cabernet and 555 the softest shiraz."

McGuigan was perceived in a very negative light by his peers, because in those days they wanted everything done in a very conservative, wine-industry way. "I received a lot of criticism," he recalls, "which was very difficult for a 30-year-old to accept, but we came through and developed companies that were significant."

At present, there are two major national and two major international wine companies with significant presence in the Hunter Valley: Orlando Wyndham, owned by Pernod Ricard, runs Wyndham Estate Winery; Mildara Blass, Australia's fourth-largest winemaker, acquired Rothbury Estate in 1996; Arrowfield in the Upper Hunter is owned by Hokuriku, a Japanese company; and Southcorp, Australia's largest winemaker, controls the Hunter labels, Lindemans, Tulloch's, Hungerford Hill and Rosemount.

"It's very obvious to me," says Patrick Auld, the former manager and chief winemaker at Lindemans, "that great fruit makes great wine and that's the challenge in this area, to make those great wines year in and year out." He should know being from a fifth-generation winemaking family on his father's side and third-generation on his mother's. After leaving school

Being maritime, the Hunter has quite high humidity, which allows the leaves to keep their pores open longer during hot weather and reduces heat stress. This allows photosynthesis and growth to continue.

he trained with Peter Lehman in the Barossa Valley, came to the Hunter Valley in 1973, worked for Brian McGuigan, and then joined Tullochs in April 1974. He was there for 27 years, through several takeovers including the most recent by Southcorp, which saw a large financial investment made to upgrade the winery.

With a move to the management side of the business, Patrick handed over production to two young winemakers. In fact, the Hunter is seeing a changing of the guard as far as winemaking is concerned. As Patrick points out, "they're very experimental, they're very creative, but at the end of the day we're here to make a product that the consumer wants to drink as well."

Although there was a time when, according to Patrick, the Hunter Valley wasn't very 'sexy', there's now a trend back to the local product. His personal vision is, "to take the Hunter back to where it was as one of the leading grape-growing regions in Australia, a producer of outstanding quality wine of styles like chardonnay, semillon, shiraz and verdelho."

A sense of history hangs about this section of the Pokolbin Valley. In 1912, Lindemans acquired Ben Ean Winery, from John McDonald, whose name the road that runs past the winery to the Hungerford Hill corner takes. Ben Ean had been established in 1870, and McDonald erected a substantial winery, which forms the central part of the present-day complex.

The direction a vineyard faces is not so critical in a warm area like the Hunter. Nevertheless, slopes provide cool air drainage at night allowing flavour and colour development to continue.

Andrew Margan is one of the new breed of vignerons who, with university training, a wealth of overseas experience and a taste for marketing, are revitalizing the Hunter Valley wine industry. Born in 1960, Andrew was virtually adopted by the Tyrrell's. "They were like another family to me," he recalls. "I grew up running around the cellar at Tyrrell's. I was plugging vats when I was about ten, as soon as I could reach the top of the vat."

Andrew did his first full-time vintage there after finishing high school, then after college Murray Tyrrell sent him to work in Bordeaux.

He came back in 1987 to work as Murray's personal assistant, and after another stint in France, he returned to become the marketing manager for Tyrrell's Wines. His four-year stint there he describes as crucial. "It taught me how we should be making wine," he admits, "instead of just thinking how you want to make wine and then seeing how the public likes it."

Andrew always had the desire to make wine, so after leaving Tyrrell's he recommissioned the old Saxonvale winery, where he and his wife Lisa did 1,500 tonnes of contract winemaking in the

first year. But that wasn't fulfilling enough so in 1997 they produced their first wine under the Margan brand. The rest is history with their semillon, merlot and chardonnay all becoming award winners.

Andrew's success is a concrete example of what new blood can do, and with the present wine boom, winemaking is also booming. Graduates of oenology from Australia and overseas are entering the industry in record numbers and bringing with them new ideas, new techniques and youthful vision.

The Hunter is benefiting from this changing of the guard. For example, at Len Evans's new vision splendid, Tower Estate, winemaker Dan Dineen is making classic regional wines by taking fruit from regions that best suit a particular grape variety.

Not all young winemakers are male or Australian, of course. Sarah-Kate Wilson was born in 1973 in the south island of New Zealand. In 1996, after completing her university training, she travelled to the Hunter to work for Iain Riggs at Brokenwood. From there, she moved to

McGuigans, and then to work on her first vintage at Wandin Valley, a name familiar to many Australians from the extremely successful soapie, *A Country Practice*. James Davern, the show's producer, bought the property and renamed it after the town in which the series was set.

"The Hunter has a feel about it," Sarah-Kate enthuses. She likes the way the young winemakers interact. "Everyone's open and friendly, but there's also that respect for the people in the industry who have been here a long time – Len Evans, the Tyrrell's – it's a good blend of young and old."

One of the former is Rhys Eather from Meerea Park who has had some success with his 1998 Alexander Munro Shiraz. Rhys has created what he calls the Young Turks, a group of young Hunter Valley winemakers who take advantage of his access to some famous old wines from Australia and abroad.

As Rhys explains, "The great winemakers of Australia probably did what we do now. They got together with people in their region, looked at the so-called great wines, and tried to work out what was happening."

With an eye to what's to come, he adds: "The Young Turks, yeah, it is the changing of the guard but it's not just the future of the Hunter Valley, it's also the future of the Australian wine industry."

The Aubrey Wilkinson vineyard (left) is situated on the historic Oakdale Property. First planted in 1866, it is widely regarded as the first vineyard in the Pokolbin area. The property was purchased by Pepper Tree Wines in 1989 and ten years later the reconstructed winery was opened, boasting the most spectacular views across the Hunter Valley. Spraying of vines (above), is essential to control the devastating effect of phylloxera.

Water is essential to the life of the vine and to repair one of the inadequacies of the Hunter, the vineyard association has developed a million-dollar pipeline from the Hunter River in to Pokolbin to provide supplementary water. Growers fill their dams from the pipeline and irrigate in times of drought.

Known for its magnificent horse studs and historic homesteads, the Upper Hunter also produces
some of the world's finest wines. The Arrowfield Winery *(above)*, carved into the hillside overlooking
the Hunter River, produces quality wines of unique character. There is no doubt that grape growing is
a capital and labour-intensive occupation, as the landscape on the right clearly indicates.

Previous pages: "The first of the blessings which nature bestows upon the more genial climates of the Earth." Extracted from James Busby's, *A Treatise on the Culture of the Vine*, 1824. *Left and above:* February and March are harvesting months and although most of the grapes are now mechanically harvested, you'll still see picking teams in the vineyards. If the weather is fine, vintage may be relaxed, if it's wet (which is often the case), all hell breaks loose.

Grape picking goes on by day at the McWilliams Mt Pleasant vineyard (*above*) and night at Tamburlaine (*right*), by hand and machine, in order to defeat the fickle nature of the weather.

This view looks over the Constable and Hershon vineyard (*left*) to the Brokenback Ridge. The vineyard totals about six hectares planted to chardonnay, cabernet sauvignon, semillon and merlot and there is also a wonderful open garden and sculpture garden. *Above:* Chris Cameron (*standing*), innovative and energetic winemaker at Pepper Tree Wines, and his staff, sampling some of their wines which are full of flavour and very accessible.

Left: Dan Dineen, young winemaker at Len Evans' vision splendid, Tower Estate Wines, operating the forklift as his assistants hand sort the grapes before they are crushed, quite a unique method in the Hunter. *Above:* Patrick Auld, former chief winemaker for Lindemans Wines for 27 years, in the barrel store at Tullochs Winery, one of the Southcorp stable of wines.

Left: Ironically, winemakers love a beer, and no more so than the Young Turks, the new breed of winemakers who gravitate to their local watering hole, Harrigans Irish Pub in Pokolbin, to share ideas, release some tension, and generally have a good time. *Above:* The winemaking establishment of the Lower Hunter: (*rear left to right*) Patrick Auld, former manager and chief winemaker of Lindemans, Bruce Tyrrell, manager of Tyrrell's Vineyards, Jay Tulloch, owner and winemaker of JYT Wine Company; (*front left to right*) Brian McGuigan, manager of McGuigan Wines, and Len Evans, wine expert and partner in Tower Estate. These five men share a unique reputation with a few others in the district. They can look back over 40 years and be proud of the contributions they have made to the reputation and status that the Hunter Valley wine industry has today.

Above: Wine tasting at Wyndham Estate, one of the many cellar doors that proliferate throughout the Hunter attracting people from all sections of society. Len Evans humorously remarked that the Hunter Valley has become Sydney's major bottle shop.
Right: The Rothbury Estate has a magnificent cask room where banquets and theatrical events are often held. Many wineries and other establishments now provide facilities for conferences and other major events to attract more people to this gastronomic theme park.

Dr Max Lake, the Sydney surgeon, *bon vivant* and former owner of Lakes Folly wrote: "Climate and drainage dominate the health of the vine, and it is one of the remarkable flukes of nature, that subtropical in latitude as much of the Hunter Valley is, the immediate growing conditions of the vine are favourable. Hickenbotham suggests the cause of this amelioration to be the fairly constant cloud cover over the area during the ripening period, January, February and March." *Following pages*: A scene that brings to mind Dr Max Lake's words: "White woollies gambol over the lion dozing at Brokenback; fierce summer breath of the tropics not far to the north; lazy hum of the cicadas; sometimes the lash of a Coral Sea cyclone."

CHAPTER FOUR

THE PEOPLE

Art, food and wine combine in
the hands of Scottish born chef,
Paula Rennger. She and her
husband Simon have brought
their unique talents to the
Hunter to entertain visitors
with a feast of original dishes
and stylish surroundings at
their restaurant, Shakey Tables.

Robert Moline, the Algerian-born owner and chef of Robert's Restaurant is reminiscing about the good old days, 30 years ago, when he was running the Hunter's first wine-country restaurant at the now defunct Saxonvale Winery. "I remember the days when all the boys, who are now very old, used to come and have lunch on the verandah of Happy Valley during vintage time. Having steak tartare – for God's sake! All of them would be showing their hands, because they were all doing the red wine and their hands were stained. They were arguing whose hands were the dirtiest. In those days, it was fantastic."

Robert, whose stepfather, Paulo, was the chef for the royal palace of Monaco, migrated to Australia in 1967, after his mother took a position with the French Consulate in Melbourne. Six years later, with his wife-to-be Sally, Robert took a drive to the Hunter Valley to escape the city and the pressures of his new restaurant at Potts Point in Sydney. There, they visited Sally's cousin and her husband, Simon Currant, the manager at the new Hungerford Hill winery. And, it was then that Robert noticed the absence of food and wine outlets, and wondered, "surely one day?"

It didn't take long for Robert's vision to be realized as, in the same year, he moved to Happy Valley Restaurant where, with his *cuisine de terroir*, Robert went on to shape the region's gastronomic identity and reputation.

His biggest achievement was Peppertree, which he created with other partners in 1991. "Peppertree became, symbolically, one little piece of land to accommodate what the Hunter Valley is best at – food and wine and hospitality," Robert proudly professes. "It's the jewel of the Hunter, it's chic, it's elegant, it's classic, it has character, it's established and it has so much history behind it." He's right about it all, including the history: the cottage where he runs the restaurant dates from 1876, the chapel from 1888, the convent is from 1909, and the winery is based on the style of those a century ago.

Robert wasn't the first and definitely not the last to be lured to the region. For some reason, Cessnock and the surrounding countryside has always attracted settlers. Since the beginning of European settlement, people keen to invest in farming, coal mining, winemaking, and now tourism, have been drawn to the area. In their wake, have followed the working classes, the Irish escaping famine and persecution, and coal miners from England, Scotland and Wales, searching for a better life on the edges of empire.

The contrast between the classes is clearly evident in their descendants. While in Pokolbin and the other winemaking areas, the lords of style and class rule their kingdoms, the town of Cessnock retains its working-class character, in its architecture, people, and attitudes. Although times are changing, the barriers still exist.

On the northern side of the Valley lives John Wright, a fifth-generation farmer, who can trace his ancestry back to the First Fleet. He owns Phoenix Park, the farms on both sides of the bridge that crosses the Hunter River at Morpeth, the former port and hub of the Hunter Valley. His great-great-grandfather led a team of convicts in the early 1820s to clear Phoenix Park, and realizing how good the land was, settled there in 1837. Recently, they drilled to find out the depth of soil and went down 18 metres before they came to rock. No wonder John's father used to call it the Garden of Eden.

John's main crop is lucerne, however, his main claim to fame is his millet brooms. As a child he remembered his father stopped growing millet because plastic brooms came on the market. Then, about 20 years ago, John planted some millet seed which grew very well. "Following an article in the local paper, a chap rang me up," recalls John, "and told me he had all the gear to make brooms. He wanted me to use it. That's how I acquired the 100-year-old machinery. Then another gentleman offered to give me lessons

Graham Doran, the vineyard supervisor for McWilliams Wines, checking the grape harvest.

on how to make brooms. I had a couple of lessons and made some funny looking brooms, but they improved and I've sort of perfected it now. If I do say so myself, I make a pretty good looking broom."

Unlike John Wright, artists Chris and Francis Fussell are recent pioneers in the district. "The day we came up in 1971," recalls Francis, "I saw kids riding their ponies along the footpath and thought this is real country, this is where I would have loved to have lived when I was a kid. It really appealed to me."

They bought a block of land in Pokolbin, and moved up from Sydney in 1975. "It was an interesting exercise for me to build my own shelter," explains Chris. "The project was to design a house from the ground up especially for this climate. It was the first mud-brick place to be built in the district."

Since those early days, Chris and Francis have established themselves as respected artists in the district, painting, sculpting and accepting commissions from many of the local establishments. Although the tourist boom has, they say, turned the area into a 'Disneyland', Francis still admits, "We've got a great life."

Another creative couple to invest in the area is Juliette Ackery, a ceramic artist, and her partner, Trevor Weekes, an 'ideas' artist, who migrated from Sydney to Wollombi, an artists' colony on the southern end of the Lower Hunter, in 1991. "We just drove into the valley one day", says Juliette. "It was spring and the whole valley was really green, lush and beautiful ... it was like a fairy dell and we were totally sucked in by the whole thing. It was like these two innocents arriving."

When Trevor had an exhibition in Sydney a few years ago, the *Sydney Morning Herald* art critic, Bruce James, commented: "Trevor is hard to categorize and I doubt very much if he cares. He is a bit of an eccentric, wandering around the landscape in board shorts and a Boy Scout hat." Trevor paints, sculpts, publishes limited-edition books, such as the *Teach A Chicken To Fly Manual,* and stages hoaxes. "I use art as a vehicle for humour," he explains, adding: "the city is no longer an option. We've been spoilt now."

Another urban refugee is organic winemaker, Roy Meyer, who danced with the Australian Ballet in the late 1950s and early '60s, before taking up a position with the Festival Ballet

in London. By 1974, accidents, age and family commitments put paid to his dancing and he became a personnel manager for Citibank in London. However, in 1983, he decided to return to Australia to look after his aging mother.

At his farewell dinner, the president of the bank asked about his future.

"I couldn't say I was going home to look after my mum," explains Roy, "so I said, completely off the top of my head, 'I'll most likely end up growing grapes in the Hunter Valley.' I didn't know where the Hunter Valley really was. The president replied, 'The Hunter Valley, that sounds like a cowboy place.'"

By 1987, Roy had fulfilled his prophecy and had taken possession of the old Saxonvale

Kevin Weldon, the Sydney publisher, appropriately attired, standing beside his French Stampe biplane, in which he performs aerobatics along with other magnificent men in their flying machines. They belong to an exclusive club of flyers who take to the air from their airfield at Lochinvar.

A team of coal miners emerging from the South Bulga underground mine after a seven-hour shift. From an area bounded by the towns of Singleton, Scone, Denman and Broke, underground and open cut mines produce more than 60-million tonnes of coal every year. The Hunter Valley has the unique reputation of producing both wine and coal for consumption by overseas markets.

winemaker's cottage and 20 acres of land, just outside Broke. So began his new occupation as an organic winemaker.

His mother was his inspiration: "She was the one who said, 'Oh, we'll find out a little bit about grapes ... I think we can do it.'"

After losing a fifth of his first plantings in 1988, Roy is now producing fine organic wines, under the Louis-Laval label, and he promotes and sells them "on the fact that my wine, in the style it is made, could have been made 100 years ago." He's passionate about his product and admits, "it's hard work but if you are connected to it, it's very, very enjoyable."

At Rothbury, on the northern edge of the Pokolbin district, Paula Rennger operates the Hunter Country Resort and Shakey Tables Restaurant with her husband Simon. Born in Edinburgh, Scotland, Paula trained as a jeweller and silversmith at the Edinburgh College of Art before migrating to Australia.

"We were looking for an opportunity," explains Paula. "This was advertised, and to

be honest, it didn't look too attractive. It was horrible." However, several years down the track, Simon and Paula have transformed what was, "a laminex-tabled, pink-chaired, fluffy-carpeted establishment," into a classy and unique resort with a reputation as one of the more progressive of the Valley's restaurants. The walls are hung with her paintings, but Paula also expresses her creative energy through her menu, using ingredients that she calls "a bit on the edge". She also likes to "break a few rules", and admits that "because of my art school background, I often work with the visual concept of how I want something to look."

The vision Paula and Simon have is to provide dining and accommodation arrangements around the wine experience. For Simon, this means providing a unique wine list of wines made from fruit grown only in the Hunter. Looking back, Paula recalls: "We didn't know an awful lot about the Hunter. We're only realizing now how lucky we are having made such a good decision. It's a really great community to be involved in."

Another couple of urban escapees are Rod and Sally Anderson who moved from Sydney to their Wollombi Brook property in 1988. After travelling and working in Europe, Sally returned to Australia where she met Rod, "and after seeing him catch a yabby, I knew he was for me". They found "the most beautiful place on Earth" where they now live what Sally calls "a very reclusive, private and passion-filled idealistic existence".

Rod is a horse whisperer, or teacher of Natural Horsemanship, as he calls it. He first became interested in this unusual career in 1989 when he met an American horse psychologist: a meeting he describes as "an epiphany". As Rod recalls, "from that moment on, that was going to be my life. I came home and found that it worked. Natural horsemanship is about self-development – you play with your horse and you work on yourself. It's not about riding, it's about relationships."

An even later arrival to the Hunter is Judy Meares who, together with her husband, returned from Hong Kong in 1995. They arrived one weekend "looking for ten acres and ended up buying 180 acres that (same) weekend." They now have 750 olive trees, ten acres of grapes, 35 cows, three donkeys and other pets, as well as an olive press – the first in the valley.

Judy's real passion, however, is theatre. For 20 years, whilst living in Hong Kong, she performed in many Broadway collections and pantomimes for an amateur theatre company. Since moving to the Hunter, Judy created Pokolbin Community Theatre in 1996 and since then, she has produced and directed several successful productions. Her aim was to "involve the Cessnock people as well as the Pokolbin people because there's a huge gap between the Cessnock coal-mining community and the vineyard-tourist people."

Judy realized that there wasn't much to do after hours. "I felt that this community theatre would involve people in an activity outside the normal," she says, "and give them something else to talk about. It gets damn boring talking about *botrytis* ('noble rot' – a wine disease)."

Her choices have been quite conscious: "I chose *Diving For Pearls*, a play about the closing of BHP in Wollongong," she admits, "because this was happening in the Hunter Valley too, particularly in Cessnock with the mine closures. And, I chose *Cosi*, a play about inmates in a lunatic asylum, also because the symbolism behind it was so strong. Everyone here spends seven days a week in the vineyards. It's just as closeted as being in a lunatic asylum."

Two young cowboys prepare for their rides at a rodeo in Cessnock. Like the miners, the rodeo riders and their audience are part of the diverse population that lives in the Hunter Valley.

Two of the Hunter Valley's original settlers: John Wright (*left*), the millet broom maker from the historic port town of Morpeth, exhibiting his handiwork, and Phil O'Connor (*above*), a local farmer, up at the crack of dawn to take his morning constitutional.

Left: Setsuko Ogishi is a Japanese-born glass artist who has been living and working in the Hunter Valley since 1987. She and her husband developed the New Hot Glass Workshop in Rothbury in 1998 and a year later opened the Ogishi Craft Centre on the same site. Setsuko is represented in many galleries and recently won the prestigious Gift Award in the Glassware Category. *Above:* Robert Molines is something of a legend in the vineyards. The Algerian-born chef is responsible for the region's gastronomic reputation, having created a number of successful restaurants in the district, using his *cuisine de terroir* philosophy. Presently he owns and runs the famous Roberts Restaurant in the beautiful setting of Peppertree, with its historic convent guesthouse and original slab homestead.

Above: Sally and Rod Anderson live in an owner-built home by the banks of the Wollombi Brook. Sally is the artist, excelling in her life studies, while her husband Rod is a horse whisperer, who uses that knowledge to help others. *Right:* Trevor Weekes and his partner Juliette Ackery moved to the village of Wollombi in 1990. Trevor is a hoax artist, who has constructed elephants with wings and illustrated books about flying pigs. *Following pages:* Francis and Chris Fussell in their mud-brick studio. Their reputation as painters and sculptors is well established in the district.

Above: Allandale's winemaker Bill Sneddon has enthusiasm, knowledge and love of his craft, which has been acquired from over 16 vintages at Allandale. A graduate of oenology from Charles Sturt University, Bill has a commitment to making wine of distinctive quality. *Right:* Andrew Margan, one of the Young Turks who cut his teeth in the business with Murray Tyrell, selected the Broke Fordwich sub-region of the Hunter Valley to plant vineyards in 1989. Andrew crafts wines of individual character and finesse that are ready to drink upon release and match perfectly with food.

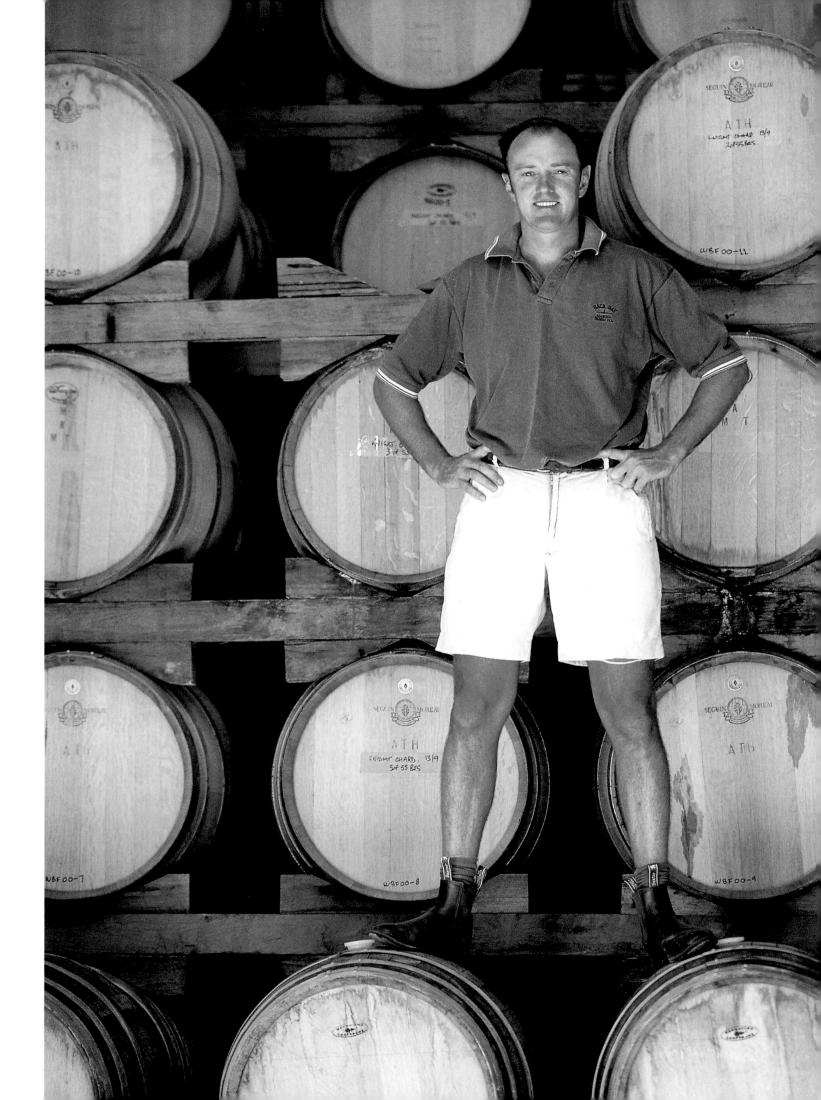

Left: Roy Meyer, the owner and winemaker of Louis-Laval wines, is a former ballet dancer who, with his chemical-free approach to farming, non-irrigation policy, and rich volcanic soil on his seven-hectare estate outside Broke, produces fruit and wines of exceptional flavour and quality. *Above:* Students at Mount View High School in Cessnock, the only high school in Australia with a viticulture course, are taught about viticulture and winemaking by their agriculture teacher in the school's own vineyard.

Left: Larry Hughes, from the small timber-mill town of Millfield, is a local musician who has lived in the Hunter all his life. He has inspired many people in the Wollombi district to take up an instrument and is very active in the cultural life of the region. *Above:* Members of the Pokolbin Community Theatre, drawn from Cessnock and the vineyards, prepare for their music hall performance in the cask room of The Rothbury Estate.

CHAPTER FIVE

THE ATTRACTIONS

Log on to the official website of Hunter Tourism and this is what you'll discover: "The Hunter Region has the best Australia has to offer, just 90 minutes drive or a half-hour flight north of Sydney. You'll find sparkling beaches, rivers and lakes ... magnificent wilderness and mountain tops. You can watch dolphins and koalas in their natural habitat or sample the Hunter's world of famous wines." Sounds like hype? Well, surprisingly it's not, it's all there and more.

Driving into Pokolbin, the centre of the wine country, is as refreshing and intoxicating as a cool glass of chardonnay. Here, you can escape from the pressures of the outside world into the corduroy-like vineyard landscapes — surely a unique experience. A maze of avenues criss-crosses the countryside, enticing you to explore further and uncover yet another cellar door, art gallery, or restaurant. At every turn a new postcard view appears. Rugged ranges encircle the valley and cool sea breezes temper the summer heat with memories of the Pacific. In the sky, hot-air balloons, tiger moths and sky divers dog fight for the best views, while on the ground, sports cars and minibuses dodge and weave through this paradise of pleasure.

Early morning joggers and walkers take advantage of the serenity of the golden sands and the freshness of the salty air at Caves Beach in the Lake Macquarie area of the Hunter.

However, there are more treats in store. Lake Macquarie, which lies about 120 kilometres north of Sydney, is the southern entrance to the Hunter. It is Australia's largest coastal lake and four times bigger than Sydney Harbour. To the west, are the Watagan Mountains and to the east is a collection of superb surfing beaches.

In the years between the wars, miners and steel workers built holiday shacks along the lake's shoreline to take advantage of the fishing, the swimming and the relaxed lifestyle. In the 1940s, William Dobell, the famous Australian artist, discovered the beauty of Lake Macquarie and escaped to Wangi Wangi, a suburb on the lake's western shore, where he lived and painted for 30 years. His timeless house is now open to the public.

Lake Macquarie is also one of Australia's yachting strongholds and on any weekend, the lake is a mosaic of sails and pleasure craft, particularly in January when it hosts the national sailing championships.

The Lake Macquarie Yacht Club at Belmont, home base of Tony Mowbray, Australia's renowned solo, round-the-world sailor, is also home to many ocean-going yachts that moor at its marina.

Further north along the Pacific Highway is the city of Newcastle, situated on the southern shore of the Hunter River. At the mouth of the river is the city's most famous landmark, Nobby's. This island houses a signal station where the harbour master overlooks the maritime traffic plying its way upriver to the bulk coal loader at Kooragang Island.

Also keeping watch over the river and the city is Fort Scratchley. Now a maritime museum that provides spectacular views of the river, the city and the Pacific Ocean, the guns of the fort have only been fired in anger once, in 1942, when they opened up on a Japanese submarine that was shelling Newcastle.

In some coastal cities, surfing may be just a subculture, but in Newcastle, it is part of the mainstream. Each summer Newcastle hosts its own festival of surfing, 'Surfest', attracting international as well as local competitors. Names, such as four-time world champion, Mark Richards, as well as Matt Hoy, Luke Egan and Nick Wood are as synonymous with Newcastle as their footballing brothers in the local rugby league team, the Newcastle Knights.

Newcastle's city beaches contribute a great deal to the city's character. The drive from Merewether Beach, through the exclusive suburb of the Hill, past Prince Edward Park, City Beach, Newcastle Baths and the Bogey Hole is one of the few remaining great coastal drives of Australia.

The city itself has undergone a remarkable transformation since that dramatic day in 1989 when Newcastle was devastated by an earthquake. Measuring 5.5 on the Richter Scale, the earthquake resulted in the deaths of 13 people, injury to more than 160, and an estimated $AU1 billion in damage.

But despite the earthquake and progress, the dominant architectural style of inner Newcastle remains an unusual mixture of Victorian and Edwardian styles. Many of these buildings have been restored, revitalizing the city and transforming inner-city suburbs such as Hamilton and Cooks Hill into vibrant, cosmopolitan centres that have become home to art galleries, restaurants and cafes.

But the catalyst for the changes that have most transformed the city's physical appearance was The Foreshore, not the earthquake. Comprising 17 hectares of harbour-front land adjacent to the CBD, it was redeveloped with government finance as part of the Australian Bicentennial in 1988. Railway yards and long-abandoned wharf areas were replaced with a harbour promenade, parklands, picnic areas, a viewing tower and the Queens Wharf, which contains bars and restaurants. The Foreshore is a focal point for locals and visitors alike.

Also part of the city's redevelopment is the Honeysuckle Project which spreads along three kilometres of harbour foreshore, creating venues for fine food markets, festivals and exhibitions.

At the northern boundary of the Hunter lies Port Stephens, a 45-minute drive north of

The Royal Australian Infantry Corps Museum in Singleton has an historically inclined collection of infantry equipment, weapons and memorabilia dating back to Australia's first overseas military excursion to the Sudan in 1885.

Newcastle. From atop the Gan Gan Lookout at Nelson Bay, the view of sheltered bays, deep anchorages and pure white beaches that comprise Port Stephens, is spectacular.

Known to locals as 'the Bay', Nelson Bay is the commercial and social hub of Port Stephens. To the south, along the Stockton Peninsula, excellent fishing and surfing spots can be found and just southwest is the Tilligerry Peninsula where a well-appointed marina makes Lemon Tree Passage a major boating centre.

The Bay's trawler fleet and oyster racks are evidence that marine life plays an important role in the community. Charter boats take amateurs out to sea for a dose of marlin, shark or yellow-fin tuna fishing, while the clear visibility and interesting reef formations make the Bay an especially attractive venue for scuba divers and snorkellers alike.

Back down the Pacific Highway and over the bridge that spans the Hunter River at Hexham, a right turn onto the New England Highway leads to Maitland, the centre of a rich agricultural area and victim of devastating floods, in 1893 and 1955. From its development in the 1830s as the major trade point for the region, Maitland soon eclipsed Newcastle in importance, and by 1850 it was considered a beautiful city, renowned for its churches and impressive buildings.

Upstream from Maitland are the riverbank towns of Morpeth, Clarence Town and Paterson, reminders of how important the river systems

The Great South Pacific Express is quintessentially an Australian train, where every detail has been sourced from Australia's railway heritage: Solid red cedar wood walls, the finest myrtle burl panels and the delicate stained glass clerestory roofs combine to make the train the most luxurious hotel on wheels. It travels north from Sydney crossing the Hawkesbury River, and arriving in the Hunter Valley en route to Brisbane, where passengers can visit the vineyards on a guided tour.

were as a transport route in the early days of the colony. The National Trust has classified Morpeth, and its setting and historical buildings imbue the town with a special character.

The Paterson Valley is one of the state's loveliest, where hazy blue mountains and richly cultivated paddocks with their tall stands of eucalypts, create an unforgettable atmosphere. Some of the small hills are crowned by old homesteads, which include some of the finest pieces of colonial architecture in the state.

Singleton, another 50 kilometres to the west, has been a prosperous rural service centre since the middle of the 19th century. However, in the second half of the 20th century, the industry base changed, as the number of open cut coal mines mushroomed. Despite this, the town still boasts many buildings of architectural and historical significance.

As you travel up the New England Highway between Singleton and Muswellbrook, coal mines and power stations dominate the landscape. Once a service centre for dairy framers and graziers, it is now home to workers in the nearby coal mines and power stations. However, many heritage buildings remain including the classic Eaton's Hotel (1857), and St. Alban's Church (1864-7), which is the work of leading English church architect, Sir Giles Gilbert Scott.

Further on, around Scone, the country is more open, the farmhouses are farther apart and there are no coal mines.

Scone is the renowned centre of Australia's thoroughbred industry where the descendants of great sires such as Todman and Star Kingdom command enormous stud fees. This prosperous

town is the centre of a wealthy district where the rich make their retreats. The most famous arrival to establish a rural domain is media magnate, Kerry Packer, who bought the historic property, Ellerston.

Another famous property, on the upper reaches of the Hunter River, is Belltrees, owned for 160 years by the White family, whose most famous son is Patrick White, the Nobel-prize-

winning author. The original homestead has been turned into a museum and a later house has become a guesthouse.

Just over the range from Belltrees, on the slopes of Mount Barrington, is another historic building – Barrington House. For many years, it has faithfully served as a holiday destination for visitors wanting to explore the wonders of the adjacent rainforests.

But by far the major tourist lure is Pokolbin and the other wine regions around Cessnock where tourist activities centre around its famous wines. Accommodation houses, restaurants and cafés, golf, galleries and gift shops, carriage rides, balloon rides and joy flights, have proliferated. The Hunter has also become a centre for music, food and harvest festivals. As the website boasts, it really does have it all.

Port Stephens is a large natural harbour, which spans the 24 kilometres between the mouth of the Karuah River to the Pacific Ocean. The area is characterized by small bays, white sandy beaches and bushland.

Above: Singleton, situated on the banks of the Hunter River, has a healthy and diverse local economy. The principal sources of income are dairying, beef cattle, viticulture, vegetable growing, coal mining, power generation, tourism, commerce and the large army base. There are 18 coal mining operations in the shire which employ 4,000 people. Singleton's fine heritage buildings embrace all the main phases of Australian architectural history, with many of the commercial and administrative buildings dating from the boom period, which ensued from the arrival of the railway in 1863. *Opposite:* The Convent Pepper Tree was built in 1909 in Coonamble, some 600 kilometres west of the Hunter Valley, for the Brigadine Order of Nuns newly arrived from Ireland. The Convent was divided into four sections and transported to its present site where it was rebuilt as faithfully as possible, even to the point of having the timber made in the same mill in Coonamble where the original timber was cut. All of the pressed metal interiors are original. Many of the walls have been moved to enlarge the rooms, which have now become elegant and luxurious suites.

Opposite: Muswellbrook is a substantial and very attractive country town of historic buildings and tree-lined streets situated beside the Hunter River. The old School of Arts is now the town hall building, which houses the Muswellbrook Regional Gallery. *Above:* The Royal Federal Hotel is one of Branxton's historic buildings. This small township, on the New England Highway between Maitland and Singleton, has several older buildings, which reflect the fact that it emerged in the early- to mid-19th century as the Hunter Valley opened up beyond Maitland.

Left: Brian Barry (in the blue shirt) conducts a course in wine appreciation at the Hunter Valley Wine School. *Above:* Jazz is a musical genre that attracts huge audiences to the Hunter Valley. Jazz in the Vines at Tyrells Long Flat attracts luminaries such as trumpeter James Morrison and reed man, Don Burroughs, while the Wyndham Estate is the venue for the Vintage Jazz Festival (*pictured above*).

High on a hill, from the distinctive Bimbadgen Estate Winery tower, you can see for miles – after all, Bimbadgen does mean lovely views. Gently rolling hills covered in manicured vineyards are set against the spectacular backdrop of the Brokenback Ranges. 'Esca Bimbadgen', an elegantly designed restaurant with a huge terrace overlooking Bimbadgen Estate's vineyards, is the perfect setting for top Sydney chef, Mark Armstrong's fine modern Australian cuisine. The Estate is also the venue for the annual Easter Sunday Blues Festival, 'Bimbadgen Blues'.

Above: Newcastle Beach lies off Shortland Esplanade which follows the coastline south from Fort Scratchley down to King Edward Park. At the northern end are the famous Newcastle ocean baths and the canoe pool, an old, large and safe children's wading pool. The southern end is noted for its surfing. Indeed the Surfest Surfing Competition is held annually on Newcastle Beach in April. *Right:* Lake Macquarie is the largest coastal saltwater lake in the Southern Hemisphere, covering 109 square kilometres (four times the size of Sydney Harbour). At the northern end, flotillas of bobbing boats and yachts with white, flapping sails crowd the waters, while fishing and swimming are also popular. At the southern end, small towns nestle into the wilderness.

Above: A very narrow finger of land extends out from the mainland at Newcastle to the knoll known as Nobbys Head whereon sits a lighthouse standing sentinel over the southern side of the Hunter estuary. Beyond the headland, the rocky mass of the southern breakwater lends a sheltering arm to ships entering the harbour. *Opposite:* Clearly visible in this picture, are the caves that give their name to Caves Beach, on the southern side of the Swansea Channel, at the entrance to Lake Macquarie.

Touring the vineyards can be a relaxing, equine experience with a number of horse-drawn carriage tours available, or you can don a motorcycle helmet and capture the scenery on the back of a tricycle with the roar of the motor and the wind in your face.

Rodeos have always been a place for people to meet and have a good time, and the Reg Lindsay Annual Wine Country Rodeo and Music Re-Union is no exception. Reg Lindsay is a legend of Australian Country Music and this is his contribution to the people of Cessnock, where he now lives.

There is always plenty of bull, plenty of clowning around, plenty of danger and
plenty of excitement at the rodeo.

Opposite: Besides the vineyards, one of the most appealing aspects of the region is the beautiful countryside.
By horseback you can personally experience the magic of the spectacular scenery and encounter the wildlife
at close hand, as is the case at Eaglereach Resort near Vacy, north of Branxton. *Above*: The sculpture at the
entrance to Wynella on the Mount View Road in Pokolbin, another centre for trail rides.

Maitland was once the principal town of the Hunter Valley and consequently it has many historic buildings of considerable quality. The railway line arrived at East Maitland in 1857 amidst much hoopla and reached West Maitland the following year. The original station was further east but the current Italianate-style building dates from about 1880. Today trains with up to 75 carriages carry coal from the open cut mines of the Upper Hunter to the bulk coal loader at Kooragang Island in Newcastle for shipment to Japan and other northern hemisphere destinations. *Following pages*: As the sun sets on a dam on the Wandin Valley Estate, nestled in the caress of gentle hills, which slope down from the rugged backdrop of the Brokenback Range, the air becomes charged and a sharp tang of pleasure permeates ones being. This is the Hunter Valley.

Suggested Reading

Riverchange, Six new histories of the Hunter, *Edited by Cynthia Hunter, published by the Newcastle Regional Library.*

Land Of Awabakal, Aboriginal Research Project Team, *published by Yarnteen Aboriginal and Torres Strait Islanders Corporation.*

A-Z of Newcastle and the Hunter, *by Norm Barney, published by Newcastle Newspapers Pty Ltd.*

Times Past in Newcastle, Lake Macquarie and the Hunter, *by Norm Barney, Published by Newcastle Newspapers Pty Ltd.*

The First 200 Years, A Hunter Pictorial with Norm Barney, *published by Hunter World Publishing.*

Historic Towns and Buildings of New South Wales, Hunter Region, *Paintings and Text by Tony Crago, Published by Ure Smith.*

A Pictorial History of Newcastle, *by John Turner, published by Kingsclear Books.*

Novocastrian Tales, *Edited by Paul Walsh, published by Elephant Press.*

Newcastle and the Hunter, The Revolution of a Region, *Managing Editor Brian Cogan, published by Focus Books.*

Journeys, The Making Of The Hunter Region, *edited by Phil McManus, Phillip O'Neill, Robert Loughran, published by Allen & Unwin.*

Hunter Wine Country, *by David Paterson, Self published.*

The Wines & History of The Hunter Valley, *by James Halliday & Ray Jarratt, published by McGraw-Hill Book Company Sydney.*

The Hunter Valley, *by Philip Cox, Howard Tanner and Meredith Walker, published by The Macmillan Company of Australia Pty Ltd.*

Hunter Wine, *by Max Lake, published by The Jacaranda Press.*

Hunter Winemakers, Their Canvas and Art, *by Max Lake, published by The Jacaranda Press.*

Classic Wines of Australia, *by Max Lake, published by The Jacaranda Press.*

Cabernet, Notes of an Australian Wineman, *by Max Lake, published by Rigby Limited.*

Mines Wines and People, A History of Greater Cessnock, *by W.S. Parkes, Jim Comerford and Dr Max Lake, published by the Council of the City of Greater Cessnock.*

Hunter Valley Wineguide, *by Nick Bulleid, published by Pizzey WIF Pty Ltd.*

Barrington Tops, A vision splendid, *by Dulcie Hartley, Self-published.*

Bushlands of the Hunter Region, *by David Waterhouse, published by Waterhouse Publications.*

Snowgums To Sand, A Guide to Port Stephens, Great Lakes, Dungog and Gloucester Region, *by Peter Jarver, published by Port Stephens Tourist Association.*

Acknowledgments

The photographers and writer would like to thank the following individuals and organizations for their generous help in the preparation of this book: Juliette Ackery, Sally & Rod Anderson, Patrick Auld, Brian Barry, Chris Cameron, Ann-Marie Cameron, Peter-James Charteris, Alison Craig-Leyland, Dan Dineen, Max Drayton, Rhys Eather, Kerry Elias, Len Evans, Jodie Evans, Don Francois, Chris and Francis Fussell, Alan Glover, Hugh Griffith, Bill Haszard, Rowena Hawkins, Brenda Ho, Huon Hooke, Larry and N'Angie Hughes, Bill and Wendy Lawson, Brad Lewis, Joan Lloyd, Ros Lyndsay, Gus Maher, Frank Margan, Andrew Margan, Clara Marosszeky, Brian McGuigan, John & Judy Mears, Roy Meyer, Paul Miley, Robert Molines, Scott & Esther O'Connell, Setsuko Ogishi, Max Patton, Simon & Paula Rengger, Iain Riggs, Phillip Ryan, Ken Sloan, Bill & Sally Sneddon, Alasdair Sutherland, Peter Torenbeek, Erica Townsend, Jay & Julie Tulloch, Bruce Tyrrell, Peter Vizzard, Desly Ward, Trevor Weekes, Kevin Weldon, Greg West, Jill White, Sarah-Kate Wilson, Richard & Lyn Woldendorp, John Wright, Vic and Sue Zielinski.

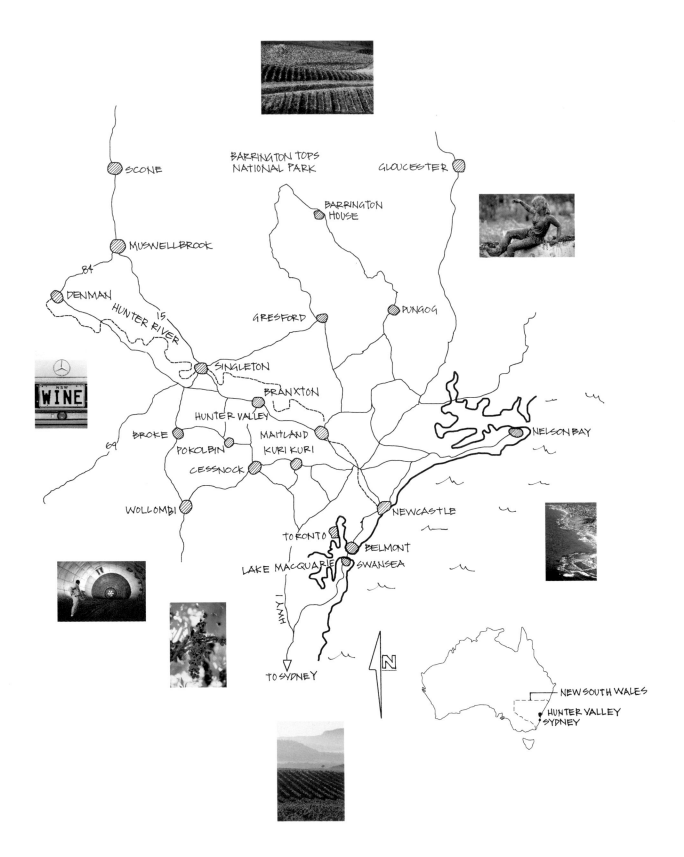

SCONE

BARRINGTON TOPS
NATIONAL PARK

GLOUCESTER

BARRINGTON
HOUSE

MUSWELLBROOK

84

DENMAN

15

HUNTER RIVER

GRESFORD

DUNGOG

WINE
NSW

SINGLETON

BRANXTON

HUNTER VALLEY

BROKE

MAITLAND

NELSON BAY

69

POKOLBIN

KURI KURI

CESSNOCK

WOLLOMBI

NEWCASTLE

TORONTO

BELMONT

LAKE MACQUARIE

SWANSEA

HWY 1

N

TO SYDNEY

NEW SOUTH WALES

HUNTER VALLEY
SYDNEY

Photography by: R. Ian Lloyd
Text by: Steve Elias
Edited by: Wendy Moore
Design Concept: Yolanta Woldendorp
Layout: Canopy Design

Hunter Valley - Australian Wine Regions was first
published in 2001 by:
R. Ian Lloyd Productions Pte. Ltd.
5 Kreta Ayer Road, Singapore 088983
Tel: (65) 227-9600 Fax: (65) 227-9363
Email: library@rianlloyd.com.sg
Website: http://www.rianlloyd.com.sg

Historical photo credits: Page 12, 16 & 17 courtesy
of the N. Barney Collection. Page 15 painting by
Joeseph Lycett reproduced with permission from
the National Library of Australia. Page 18 & 19
by Max Dupain courtesy of Jill White. Page 20
courtesy of the Newcastle Herald.

Map on Page 140 by Kevin Sloan

This book is available for bulk purchase for sales
promotion and premium use from
R. Ian Lloyd Productions Pte. Ltd.

Distributed in Australia by:
Tower Books Australia
PO Box 213, Brookvale
NSW, 2100, Australia
Phone: (61) 2 9975 5566
Fax: (61) 2 9975 5599

Printed in Singapore using the computer to plate
process by Tien Wah Press Pte. Ltd.
ISBN No. 981-04-4312-9
10 9 8 7 6 5 4 3 2 1